W9-CCX-909

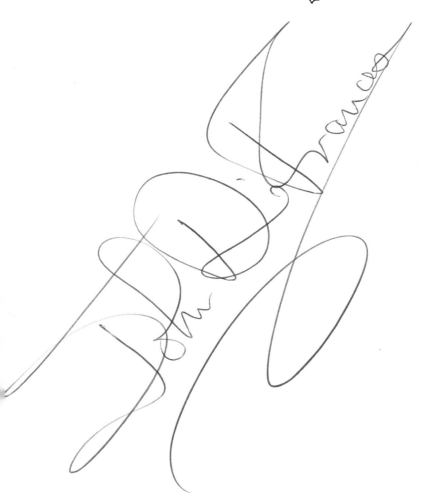

WHAT OTHERS ARE SAYING...

"Powerful...a much-needed answer for today's corporate crisis."
~ **Ken Blanchard, coauthor,** *The One Minute Manager®*
and *Whale Done!*™

"...Let's all read *Reclaiming the Ethical High Ground!* It may just
be that our intense world of 'Quarterly Earnings Reports' has left
us no time to re-evaluate our values. John Di Frances has placed
a mirror in front of us with a challenge to raise the bar for ethical
standards, while at the same time, repave the road toward the
organization of character and values. That, Ladies and
Gentlemen, is the formula for permanent (not quarterly)
success!... Great insight!"
~ **Horst H. Schulze, CEO, West Paces Hotel Group**
(Former CEO, The Ritz Carlton Hotel Company)

"In his book, *Reclaiming the Ethical High Ground*, John
Di Frances speaks passionately and eloquently about the need for
a revitalization in American business ethics. He posits that it is
only by taking the high ground as an organization of character that
companies can clear the soil for true growth and sustainable
shareholder value. This is how the real battle is won. *Reclaiming
the Ethical High Ground* is not only timely, it's timeless."
~ **Edward Emma, President, Jockey International**

"The need for this book is obvious and the timing is perfect.
Every day we are reading about a scandal involving some
previously respected company. *Reclaiming the Ethical High
Ground* is a refreshing look at important truths. After forty-six
years in business and fourteen as a CEO, I can recommend this
book to all who would like to be the great leaders of the future."
~ **Wes Cantrell, Retired Chairman and CEO**
Lanier Worldwide Inc.

"The book provides a principle-centered approach to solving ethical problems that any decision maker would do well to reflect upon."
  ~ Gerald Heinz, Corporate Counsel, Snap-on Incorporated

"John convinces us that the high road is the only one with a direct path to sustainable profit and legacy. *Reclaiming the Ethical High Ground* is a 'must read' for leadership teams committed to excellence."
  ~ Roxanne Emmerich, Author of *Thank God It's Monday: How to Build a Motivating Workplace*

"*Reclaiming the Ethical High Ground* offers a clear and simple prescription for success; create organizations with high ethical character. John Di Frances provides refreshing clarity in today's cloudy business climate."
  ~ Larry Julian, Author of *God is My CEO*

"Excellent resource! ...Empowering information for the corporate world. *Reclaiming the Ethical High Ground* presents executives with a comprehensive and practical plan for raising the ethical standard."
  ~ Jim Cerroni, Vice President of Sales, Kapro Industries - U.S.A., (Formerly Global Training Director, Milwaukee Electric Tool, Inc.)

"John Di Frances delivers! ...Practical, no-nonsense solutions to the current ethical crisis. A powerful wake-up call to corporate America...*Reclaiming the Ethical High Ground* is a must-read for all business leaders."
  ~ Guy Conn, Pastor, Fox River Christian Church

"A very good book, a very good read, very insightful...a great reminder of how to do business."
  ~ Robert Huette, President, Southwest Rail Industries

"Character has always been the most important attribute of leadership. Likewise, integrity must embody the culture of a corporation for it to succeed long-term. Together, they inspire confidence in the marketplace and in society, and positive direction for employees. John's newest book, *Reclaiming the Ethical High Ground: Developing Organizations of Character* emphasizes the importance of this principle."
~ Archie Dunham, Chairman & CEO, Conoco Inc.

"Business Ethics and material rewards have always been in conflict. It's time to reclaim the High Ground—let this generation turn the ethical tide. John Di Frances' value system and beliefs are well reflected in this book—let's not walk away from this one. Read *Reclaiming the Ethical High Ground*."
~ Frank M. Zenobia Jr., President, Zenobia & Associates, Inc., Business Integration

"Wow, what a great read...I especially like the use of all the examples, from Buford to Buffett, history continues to prove these points."
~ Randy Hennen, Publisher, Hennen Publishing

Rating: "!!!! Exceptional..."
(This rating represents the top ten percent of books published and distributed in America each year.)
~ "Best Reads"
Today's Books

"...Reclaiming the Ethical High Ground is a very much-needed antidote for today's climate of corporate scandals and should be required reading by anyone having responsibility for the corporate health of their company whether it is local, regional, national, or international in scope."
~ "Small Press Watch"
The Midwest Book Review

RECLAIMING

THE

ETHICAL HIGH GROUND

RECLAIMING

THE

ETHICAL HIGH GROUND

Developing Organizations of Character

JOHN DI FRANCES

Reliance Books ◆ Wales, Wisconsin

Reliance Books
208 E. Oak Crest Drive, Suite 250
Wales, WI 53183-9700 U.S.A.
Tel: (262) 968-9857   Fax: (262) 968-9854
http://www.reliancebooks.com   contact@reliancebooks.com

ORDERING INFORMATION

Quantity sales: Special discounts are available on quantity purchases by corporations, associations, and others. For details, contact the "Special Sales Department" at the Reliance Books address above.

Individual sales: Reliance Books publications are available at most bookstores. They can also be ordered direct from Reliance Books: Tel: (262) 968-9857; Fax: (262) 968-9854; www.reliancebooks.com

Printed in the United States of America

Publisher's Cataloging-in-Publication
(Provided by Quality Books, Inc.)

Di Frances, John.
Reclaiming the ethical high ground : developing organizations of character / John Di Frances.
    p. cm.
Includes bibliographical references and index.
LCCN 2002110231
ISBN 0-9709908-1-2

1. Business ethics. 2. Industrial management--Moral and ethical aspects.
I. Title.

HF5387.D54 2002   174'.4
                         QBI02-200567

This book is dedicated to the memory of Paul Pelczynski and John Scigliano, two wonderful friends and businessmen of true character and integrity, both of whom lost their lives recently through tragic accidents.

ACKNOWLEDGEMENTS

The undertaking of writing a book requires not only the commitment of the author, but also of all the people involved in the author's life. This book would not have been possible without their support and understanding.

I especially want to thank a number of individuals, beginning with my family, who endured the long evenings and weekends when I laybored over the keyboard. My wife, Sally, who, together with my daughter Christy, are the most exacting English scholars I know, and also two of the most unrelenting editors. Forgive me for my impatience during the repeated rewrites. I love ideas and their expression, but grow impatient with the slow, tedious process of reworking each word until it shines. Also, my daughter Annie, who has been a joy to work with in the firm and who labored so long and hard to design the book and cover. Lastly, thanks to Jamie, Joshua and Sarah, who allowed me the freedom to write what I believe was a book that had to be written for the sake of our heritage as a free people.

I also want to express my gratitude to Nancy Miskelley, Michelle Gugin and Chris Unholz of my staff, who held the fort and covered for me when necessary so that this book could be completed, especially in the final days of manuscript editing. Your support formed a crucial link in making this book happen. And finally, to several old and new friends, who have been a continuing source of encouragement through the years: Bill Rozga, an honorable man in business and personal life, David York, who has always had faith in what I wanted to accomplish and, most recently, Frank Zenobia, who came alongside near the end, when my strength was flagging, to be a source of enormous encouragement.

Thank you to everyone involved in the production of this book. Without your help, it would still be just a manuscript. Finally, I am grateful to those who read the early drafts and lent their endorsement to my thoughts.

TABLE OF CONTENTS

CONTENTS

There can be no other solution to the problem of restoring confidence aside from effective leadership fully committed to maintaining high ethical standards.

~ JOHN DI FRANCES

PREFACE

[preface]

Why the HIGH GROUND of ETHICAL CHARACTER?

reface

Preface

Survival—a foremost concern for every corporate CEO in America. The days we live in are like standing on a busy street during an earthquake. Between tremors, one can only wonder which buildings will fall next. Our economy had yet to recover from September 11th when, to make matters worse, the Enron debacle hit. This was followed by the domino effect of Global Crossing, Qwest, WorldCom and a host of others. The breach of trust has now spread beyond the corporate community to infect the very watchdogs of corporate financial probity itself, the international auditing firms. This disgrace has resulted in such erosion of public trust in our corporate entities that the general populace, as well as the investment community and capital markets, are left questioning which public companies' audited statements can now be relied upon as a basis for investment.

In his speech to Wall Street, President George W. Bush decried the growing corporate disrepute by saying, "The business pages of American newspapers should not read like a scandal sheet. The American economy today is rising, while faith in the fundamental integrity of American business leaders is being undermined. Nearly every week brings better economic news, and a discovery of fraud and scandal."[i]

A Clear *and* Present Danger

Investors are running scared—and with good reason. In order to invest prudently, they need reliable financial information, and the sole source for that information is the corporations themselves and their auditors. Former Chairman of the Federal Reserve, Paul A. Volcker, has observed that the current state of accounting and business "poses a clear and present danger to the effectiveness and efficiency of capital markets. People now don't have faith and reasonable confidence in financial reporting. That affects

19

the flow of capital, and ultimately it could affect the amount of capital that's available to business. In a capitalist system, that's not good."[ii]

Mr. Volcker is not alone in voicing such dire concerns. Mr. William George, former Chairman and CEO of Medtronic has said, "The erosion of investor confidence really worries me... If you think about it, the whole capitalist system is built upon investor confidence.... There is more at stake here than how CEOs feel about this. The whole capitalist system is at stake here."[iii]   Mr. Scott Cleland, CEO of the Precursor Group, which advises investors stated, "We have a deep crisis in confidence."[iv]

Solution *to the* Confidence Crisis...

The only way to ensure that the financial information being reported is thoroughly accurate is for Senior Executives and Boards of Directors to publicly embrace a much higher standard of integrity and personal accountability than has been exhibited in the past. There can be no other solution to the problem of restoring confidence aside from effective leadership fully committed to maintaining high ethical standards. The President reinforced this point by saying, "Our economy and our country need...confidence in the character and conduct of all of our business leaders...I am calling for a new ethic of personal responsibility in the business community—an ethic that will increase investor confidence, make employees proud of their companies and regain the trust of the American people."

Timely action in establishing this paradigm will not only restore confidence in our public corporations and free market system, it will also assure improved communication, deepen trust, and instill a renewed sense of purpose within the organization itself. This is the tried and true formula for success. Reclaiming the high ground of strong ethical leadership is not only the most certain formula for long term success, but it also represents the first step in developing an organization of character.

What do we mean by the expression "ethical high ground"? High ground represents a place where the air is clear and the view of surrounding activity unobstructed. High ground offers the strategic advantage of not having to fight uphill. It is also a vantage point from which one can see above the smoke, noise, and clutter of the surrounding battlefield to make wise decisions. High ground provides essential clarity for success, not only on a military battlefield, but also on the raging battlefield of business. In the corporate business world, the high ground is moral rather than physical. Though one is tangible and the other abstract, the stakes are just as critical.

Leaders Must Stand Firm

Some leaders may be wondering if it is even possible, wise, or in the best interest for a corporation's long term prospects and profitability to reclaim the ethical high ground? The answer is a resounding "Yes"! However, if we are to secure this ethical high ground for ourselves and our organizations, we must be prepared to pay a personal cost as leaders by exercising the moral fortitude to stand firm no matter how risky or unpopular our position may be at times. As Harry Truman said, "The buck stops here!"

Confident that in the long run, right will ultimately prevail; he faced difficulty unafraid, taking long views of life and continuing, as Emerson has said, "to believe what the centuries say against the years and the hours."

~ From the biography of
HARVEY S. FIRESTONE

CHAPTER ONE

[chapter]

I

THE MORAL DILEMMA:

WHAT'S AT STAKE?

CHAPTER ONE

What's at stake in the battle for the ethical high ground? Everything. Everything we depend upon in our capitalist, free enterprise system. We stand today at the brink of a full scale "corporate leadership credibility crisis." *BusinessWeek* recently stated: "Things have gotten so bad that even CEOs untouched by scandal—the overwhelming majority—are feeling tainted."[v] Henry M. Paulson, Chairman and CEO of Goldman Sachs, told the National Press Club that, "I cannot think of a time when business overall has been held in less repute." He went on to state that this lack of faith in our corporate leaders was a factor forestalling recovery in the financial markets.[vi] John Snow, CEO of CSX Corporation recently said, "All of us feel tarnished by much of what has gone on."[vii] And Treasury Secretary Paul O'Neill expressed his sentiments bluntly when he remarked, "I think anyone who's paying attention ought to be outraged about the things that keep tumbling out...."[viii] This is not what we think is responsible behavior."[ix]

Business *is about* Trust

If one reduces all of business to its lowest common denominator, it is not about sales or profits, but trust—the bedrock of commerce. Business is built upon relationships, and these relationships rely upon trust. In the most basic economies, village people buy, sell and barter with those they know and trust. Our economy is built upon this same simple model, yet because of widespread trust it has been able to develop into a much more sophisticated transactional form.

Corporations spend billions of dollars annually on advertising their products and services. Why? Certainly they desire to make customers aware of these products and services, but there is also the ever-important goal of building name and brand recognition, as these serve to establish trust.

When purchasing any product or service, which are you more likely to choose—a brand that you have never heard of or one that is familiar? Naturally, you prefer the one you know. For this reason, corporations augment their direct advertising budgets with prodigious spending on public relations campaigns. PR is not directed at selling any specific product or service, but merely reinforcing a corporate name, image, logo or slogan in order to favorably predispose us to a specific company at a time when we are ready to buy.

Without Trust, Markets Break Down

Without trust, even the most basic of village markets breaks down. In such a marketplace, if I distrust you, I will extend my money to you with one hand only as my other hand lays hold of the chicken I am buying. Such a basis for commerce does not operate well even in a primitive economy and will not function at all in our complex marketplace. In doubt? Take a moment to recall what happened to Firestone's tire sales following their botched handling of the Ford Explorer SUV tire problem in 2001, when Firestone attempted to deny tire design defects and transfer all responsibility to Ford.

Contrast Firestone's recent actions with the attitudes of its founder. The following is taken from a book in my library entitled simply *Harvey S. Firestone 1868-1938*.

> Mr. Firestone was a deeply religious man. Here was the fundamental source of his strength—his belief on God, and his faith in his fellowmen. He never doubted this is a moral universe in which spiritual values are supreme. Confident that in the long run, right will ultimately prevail; he faced difficulty unafraid, **taking long views of life and continuing, as Emerson has said, "to believe what the centuries say against the years and the hours."**[x]   *(Emphasis added)*

Harvey Firestone believed in handling problems in a principled manner. He was a man of honor and good character. The present leadership of the Firestone Tire Company and its Japanese parent, Bridgestone, would have benefited from reading this biography before responding as they did to the recent tire crisis.

Trust builds confidence, which facilitates our ability to transact business across time and distance without relying upon face-to-face personal knowledge and friendship as a prerequisite for each transaction. Likewise, a lack of trust breeds doubt and fear, which impedes business transactions and causes us to pull back. Although circumstances were different, a disaster similarly rooted in mistrust took place in the Silver Panic of 1893.[xi] On August 8th of that year, at a special session of Congress called specifically to deal with the resulting crisis of financial confidence, President Grover Cleveland began his address with the following comments:

> Our unfortunate plight is not the result of untoward events or conditions related to our natural resources, nor is it traceable to any of the afflictions which frequently check national growth and prosperity. With plenteous crops, with abundant promise of remunerative production for manufacture, with unusual invitation to safe investment, and with satisfactory assurance to business enterprise, suddenly financial distrust and fear have sprung up on every side. Numerous moneyed institutions have suspended because abundant assets were not immediately available to meet the demands of frightened depositors. Surviving corporations and individuals are content to keep in hand the money they are usually anxious to loan, and those

engaged in legitimate business are surprised to find that the securities they offer for loans, though heretofore satisfactory, are no longer accepted. **Values supposed to be fixed are fast becoming conjectural, and loss and failure have invaded every branch of business.**[xii]

(Emphasis added)

Business *requires* Trust
Trust *requires* Constancy

Trust is based on constancy. Constancy can only result from a faithful adherence to fixed ethical standards. When we have a high level of assurance that the leadership of an organization will not "cook the books" or engage in other dubious accounting practices to inflate financial performance and when we can be certain that their auditors will not pass on any questionable accounting practices, then we have trust. Why? Because we know the standard and have faith that it is neither changing nor subjective. It is a standard fixed in place and time, not to be altered for expediency, the economy, or any other factor.

In our economic system, it is trust that is ultimately at stake. And such trust is an absolute prerequisite if we are to prosper within a free economic system.

31

If we are to continue to prosper as a nation and to remain a model for the rest of the world to follow in developing free societies and economies based on trust, then we must return to valuing personal and corporate integrity above financial gain.

~ JOHN DI FRANCES

CHAPTER TWO
[chapter]

II

FALLEN GIANTS:
HOW DID WE GET HERE?

CHAPTER TWO

Perhaps we should ask ourselves, "What course propelled us into our current ethical crisis?" First of all, does it matter? Yes, it does. For if we do not understand the market forces at work, how can we arrive at an effective solution? The issue of responsibility demands that we look at all aspects of our present corporate and capital market ethics dilemma.

It is easy to place responsibility for these ethical lapses on corporate leaders, especially when their annual economic fortunes rise and fall by millions of dollars with their organization's reported financial results. Truth be told, in many instances a CEO's ego is as much a driving factor as remuneration. Taken together, these two forces serve as a strong impetus to "make the plan numbers" and pacify clamoring investors regardless of reality.

Keepers *of the* "Gold Standard"

Functioning alongside the corporations are the international audit firms—long standing names that, until recently, were highly regarded as the watchdogs of public companies in particular, as well as of privately held concerns. Their function was to pass upon the validity of the results being reported by a company. In effect, they were the keepers of the "gold standard." In this manner, each enterprise was measured against the same standard, thereby allowing capital investors to compare not only the relative results of one corporation against another, but also to gauge the relative risk factors associated with anticipated financial rewards for investing.

Auditing is an old practice and one to which great respect and stature were once ascribed. Names like Arthur Andersen resonated in mahogany paneled boardrooms with a hushed awe for good reason. The major accounting firms, once known as the "Big 8," were trusted internationally. In fact, a recent article in The *Wall Street Journal* recounted this heritage in their unique role as watchdogs over corporate integrity.

> A display in the Andersen Heritage Center is devoted to yellowing press clippings of a long-ago campaign to clean up the accounting industry by Leonard Spacek, who led the firm from 1947 to 1963. In one, he accused Bethlehem Steel of overstating its profits in 1964 by more than 60%. In another, he bashed the Securities and Exchange Commission for failing to crack down on companies that cooked their books, saying that at best the regulatory agency has been "a brake on the rate of retrogression in the quality of accounting."[xiii]

Regrettably, in some audit firms a decade of fast fortunes from high-flying consulting contracts, dwarfing annual audit incomes, has shattered this sterling image. Enticed by the promise of ever more lucrative and "sexy" projects, audit firms and their partners committed the unthinkable. They decided the grass was indeed greener on the other side of the fence, in fact, on both sides! First, they devised schemes allowing their clients to circumvent the rules; then they audited the same clients' compliance to those "rules."

In response to this issue, Paul A. Volcker has noted,

> Auditors have not been able or willing to exercise discipline in an environment that's extremely difficult. Accounting standards themselves have not kept up with business practices. And the stock market boom created enormous wealth—and enormous pressure to manage earnings and keep up the growth. These all led to pressures that were inconsistent with the executives' and auditors' responsibilities.[xiv]

Fox Guarding the Hen House

The seductive world of creative financial consulting has come at a very high price to audit firms. Loss of objectivity became the first casualty. In many cases, this was soon followed by a loss of freedom in questioning a client's dubious accounting practices. Having the same firm design new and innovative financial techniques and subsequently audit the results invariably places the fox in charge of guarding the hen house. How can an auditor disapprove of the practices instituted at the client corporation by his own firm? In the manufacturing sector, this would equate to the quality assurance department establishing manufacturing processes and schedules for production and then inspecting the goods produced to those processes rather than to the customer's specifications. Although not impossible, this arrangement certainly creates a strong conflict of interest.

If some corporate executives and audit firms are to be condemned for their role in the current ethical crisis, the stock analysts and their firms must also share responsibility. Merrill Lynch has recently agreed to pay $100 million and to change the manner in which it monitors and pays its analysts. This settlement resulted from a New York State Attorney General's investigation into the conduct of our nation's largest brokerage firm in issuing research reports about the outlook for the stock of its investment banking clients. It is likely that both the State of New York and the Securities and Exchange Commission will also pursue investigations of similar conduct at other brokerage firms.[xv]

It is a sad commentary that some brokerage firms and their analysts think they are insulated from the problem. Corruption is inevitable when money becomes the first priority. The President has said, "Stock analysts should be trusted advisers, not salesman with a hidden agenda. We must prevent analysts from touting weak companies because they happen to be clients of their own firm for underwriting or merger advice. This is flat-out conflict of interest...."[xvi]

Spinning Straw *into* Gold

Added to this milieu is the investor, both institutional and individual, bent on spinning straw into gold. The long-lived expansion of the 1990s generated a surreal expectation that price, earnings and value were no longer directly related, as well as the absurd notion that markets must continue their upward trend forever, irrespective of world events. William George commented, "...There has been a tremendous pressure to meet expectations or beat them rather than to produce good long-term results. It's unrealistic to think that one corporation can do that every quarter forever because there are things that happen to companies. This has pushed financial logic to an extreme."[xvii]

Consequently, a climate was created rewarding those companies that could perpetuate these grand expectations and swiftly punishing those that could not. When long-term results are judged not by decades or even years, but rather by mere monthly and quarterly statements, anxious analysts and investors offer little forgiveness for companies that cannot achieve spectacular results every quarter, without fail and without regard for market conditions far outside of the control of corporate leaders.

Recounting *the* Bodies

I am reminded of the expectations of the Johnson administration during the course of the Vietnam War. Due to enormous media pressure for battlefield successes on a daily basis, the U.S. military soon came to understand that each day must begin with enemy body counts from the prior day's fighting that greatly outnumbered the U.S. casualties. It did not take too long before military leaders learned to deliver the demanded results, no matter how many times the enemy dead needed to be recounted.

In every endeavor of life, when we insist that our desires become the reality, we shed great and valuable protections and place ourselves at enormous risk. Wishful thinking does not make it so. The fairy tale emperor's "new clothes" are just as vaporous today. We cannot exchange euphoric market expectations for reality without great harm to our free market system.

Long-Term *vs.* Fast Buck

William George eloquently addressed the investor greed

issue by stating that,

> [He would advise investors] to put their money into companies that they are confident are well governed and well run and to look at the long-term results— not just whether the company is meeting analysts' expectations.
>
> This is not necessarily going to appeal to an investor that wants a gain in a one-week or one-month period, but to someone who is looking at a five to 10-year period. This is how good companies are run: with leadership principles and good governance.[xviii]

After all, isn't investment in the stock of corporations supposed to reflect a long-term investment strategy versus "fast-buck," day-trading mentality? Due in large part to the growth of our economy during the past several decades, over 50% of American families now own stock in corporations, either directly, or indirectly through pension funds and insurance policies. Much of this wealth is in the form of retirement savings. Over the past year, these investors have watched their savings vanish.

As we have become a nation of investors, we share a common outrage at the stunning abuses that have recently been disclosed within the corporate sector. Manipulating stock prices and "ripping-off" publicly traded companies has become tantamount to stealing from the public treasury! Both corporate executives and investors must re-think their motivations.

Achievement requires
Time,
Patience,
& Commitment

Greed and selfish ambition are bad for America and our personal pocketbooks. We need to return to a mindset that seeks real growth over the long-term and reinvestment by our corporations back into the economy through stable employment growth and the development of responsible relationships with companies' employees, customers and suppliers. Achieving this takes time, patience and a commitment to doing what is right.

Since World War II, America has served as both the economic engine and model for the world. Economies world-wide have repeatedly looked to the U.S. to pull them out of recession. Moreover, much of the world has to a large extent adopted our system of free market enterprise as their guide to achieving sustainable prosperity. Recent events have not only tarnished our image worldwide but the market turmoil here has reverberated around the globe, diminishing confidence in the American capitalist system as the paradigm to follow.

At the very time our President has been asking other nations to join with us in a great moral crusade against the tyranny of extremism and terror, at considerable cost to their own economies and national security, we have demonstrated to the world our own inability, at least by a notable few, to rein in greed and selfishness.

We live in a highly charged and dangerous world. The present threat of terrorism escalated to a level of open warfare, the ongoing Arab-Israeli conflict, the tinder-keg risk of all-out nuclear war between India and Pakistan, as well as numerous less publicized wars and uprisings plaguing Africa and other parts of the world are likely to continue in the foreseeable future. Immense economic hardship already afflicts numerous developing countries whose national economies teeter on the brink of collapse. Our present economic troubles only serve to intensify these global problems and diminish our nation's leadership role at a time when strong moral leadership and the hope of improving economic conditions are desperately needed everywhere.

No Capitalism *without* Conscience

The conduct of our corporate leaders extends far beyond their boardrooms, employees, stockholders, customers and vendors. Their actions impact our nation and the world. William Hickey, CEO of Sealed Air Corporation, put it curtly when he said, "People who rob banks go to jail; people who rob shareholders should, too."[xix] As President Bush has stated, "In the long run there's no capitalism without conscience. There is no wealth without character."[xx]

If we are to continue to prosper as a nation and to remain a model for the rest of the world to follow in developing free societies and economies based on trust, then we must return to valuing personal and corporate integrity above financial gain. If they serve no other purpose, our fallen giants at least should teach us this lesson.

Character is the single most important ingredient for leadership.

~ GENERAL H. NORMAN SCHWARZKOPF

CHAPTER THREE

[chapter]

III

THE ANTIDOTE:

A VIABLE SOLUTION

CHAPTER THREE

I s there an antidote to this sickness, a viable solution to moral erosion? Yes—one that has stood the test of time. What's more, this solution is not difficult to understand or implement organization-wide, although it does demand a price. It is strong, but not inflexible. It is resourceful, but not devious; powerful, but not arrogant. Character. An old-fashioned word to some, but nonetheless pertinent today. General H. Norman Schwarzkopf has stated: "Character is the single most important ingredient for leadership." No statement could be closer to the mark.

In the wake of the Enron, Andersen, Global Crossing, Qwest, WorldCom and other debacles, cries of "foul play" fill the media. As a result, elected officials play into the public outcry, and are busy once again rewriting the accounting disclosure laws that affect public companies. The question remains: Will stiffer criminal penalties, new regulations and increased oversight prevent the next episode of corporate wrongdoing? Regrettably, they will not.

On June 14, 2000, the Securities and Exchange Commission brought civil and administrative fraud charges against seven former officials of CUC International and Cedant Corporation for their involvement in a massive financial fraud which resulted in billions of dollars of investor losses. This fraud had begun in the 1980s with the merger of CUC and HFS Incorporated and continued until April 1998, when it was finally discovered.

As he announced these charges, the SEC's Enforcement Director, Richard H. Walker said,

> Today's actions make crystal clear that the SEC and the U.S. Attorney have zero tolerance for fraudulent financial reporting. Financial fraud causes grave harm to the investing public and

undermines the integrity of our capital markets. Investors need to know that when they invest their hard-earned dollars in a company's stock, they can depend on the reliability and accuracy of the financial information that the company reports about its operations. We will continue to do everything we can to give them that confidence.[xxi]

Although I am certain that Mr. Walker had the highest intentions and was absolutely committed to his statement, such well-intentioned policies have unfortunately done little to curb the rampant financial reporting fraud, now so glaringly evident. The SEC and the U.S. Attorney will undoubtedly prosecute to the fullest extent possible, given their resource constraints, any companies found violating the law in this regard, but the resources of both organizations have been stretched razor thin. The SEC is overwhelmed by the sheer number of public company and broker frauds each year, and the events of September 11, 2001, have caused the Justice Department to focus its attention predominantly on violent crime, illicit drugs and terrorist activity, rather than on corporate white collar financial fraud. New regulations, particularly increased enforcement and harsher criminal penalties, although necessary, will not solve the present credibility crisis.

Is new legislation the answer?

The true question is not whether corporate America needs legislative changes, but rather, when will corporate leaders address the real issue, namely a commitment to *Developing Organizations of Character?* The fact is that neither external regulation and enforcement nor internal policy statements alone will solve the problem. Returning to the insightful remarks of Paul A. Volcker, "Corporate responsibility is mainly a matter of attitudes, and the attitudes got corrupted by the mentality in the markets in the 1990s. We went from 'greed is good' being said as a joke to people thinking that 'greed is good' was a fundamental fact."[xiv] Mr. Andrew S. Grove, Intel's current Chairman and former CEO stated, "I've been in business for 40 years—25 or 30 years in senior management and I find myself feeling embarrassed and ashamed by what I see in corporate America."[xxii]

Nothing short of a top-down commitment to the imperative of excellent ethical character will do, because no company will ever successfully change its behavior until the senior leadership adopts and upholds ethical attitudes. Granted, we can never eliminate all corporate wrongdoing simply because we will never convince every corporate leader, manager, and employee that integrity comes before profits. However, if honest businesses implement this higher standard, it is possible to prevent the recurrence of large scale corporate fraud and misconduct.

We must also recognize that this is not just a North American issue. The greed and deception that led to the downfall of both Enron and Arthur Andersen are alive and well worldwide. In Europe, for example, I am currently aware of another major international accounting firm whose offices on the continent are experiencing a sudden influx of new clients as corporations flee the sinking Andersen ship. On the one hand, the firm gladly welcomes all of its newfound clients, while on the other hand, the firm's partners are just now shoring up similar "Andersenesque" breaches within their own organization.

How can character-based organizations effectively prevent recurrences of ethical bankruptcy and business loss? In the case of Enron, or even Andersen for that matter, if just one senior official with knowledge of the wrongdoing had demonstrated moral fiber, he or she could have exposed the entire "house of cards." This revelation should have occurred long before matters escalated into the avalanche that economically ruined tens of thousands of Enron employees, investors, and suppliers alike, as well as substantially damaging thousands of Andersen partners worldwide, despite the fact that the majority had no hand in the deception.

An unsullied reputation greatly improves your prospects in any marketplace. In essence, when you develop an organization of character, you profoundly enhance your company's economic and professional standing as well as invest in its long-term future prospects.

But why has a lack of ethics so permeated the business environment? Certainly, some executives have chosen to "steal" all they could get their hands on regardless of moral or legal constraint. Though of the white-collar variety, they are still very much criminals. These miscreants are by far the exception. Fortunately, a large number of executive leaders have consistently refused to compromise. But what about those executives who have quietly given ground by participating in or acquiescing to the accounting shenanigans that have now compelled hundreds of companies to restate their prior years' earnings?

The Big Lie...

Thirty years of business experience has, for me, confirmed

that the vast majority of business men and women have no wish to compromise in areas they consider to be unethical. If that is the case, why is it happening? I believe that many business leaders have been taken in by the prevalent view, which regards ethical compromise as a necessary evil for their organization to remain competitive and viable. This is a lie. Compromise is not a prerequisite for success. There are companies all across America and the globe in virtually every industry that have chosen not to compromise their ethics. They still experience excellent growth and generate a satisfactory profit.

Compromise is
Not
a prerequisite for success.

I can think of no better starting point than that of Arthur Andersen, which until a few months ago was the largest audit firm in the world and is now virtually defunct. What the entire world knows today is that Andersen ended in a monumental collapse, brought about by ethical failure—a tragic ending to a company which began so well. Few people know that Arthur Andersen, the man, founded and built the firm based upon a staunchly uncompromising ethical standard. A recent article in The *Wall Street Journal* related the following from the firm's past:

> Arthur Andersen himself originally built his business
> by putting reputation over profit. In 1914, months
> after the 28-year-old Northwestern University
> accounting professor founded his tiny company, the
> president of a local railroad demanded that he
> approve a peculiar transaction that would have
> lowered the company's expenses and boosted
> earnings. Mr. Andersen, who at the time was
> worried about meeting his next payroll, told the
> president that there was 'not enough money in the
> city of Chicago' to make him do it, according to a
> book published by the firm in 1988. The client
> promptly fired the accountant, but Mr. Andersen
> was vindicated months later when the company filed
> for bankruptcy.[xxiii]

The railroad company was, in effect, a 1914 version of
"Enron." The enticement—the same, namely the
restatement of earnings by hiding expenses and losses. For
Mr. Andersen, integrity was a matter of principle, an
indispensable priority. He would not yield. By contrast,
his modern counterpart, Arthur Andersen corporation,
took the bait, because money meant more than honor. If

Andersen had spurned Enron's overtures in the late 1990's, they would undoubtedly still be in business today. Ironic isn't it? Arthur Andersen's fledgling business risked all for integrity. The multinational corporation, his namesake, lost all for the lack of it.

But what about today? Are there numerous examples of corporate executives who daily reject the relativism so pervasive in some organizations and still build prosperous enterprises? The answer unequivocally "yes"! Many, many of them. The list below names only a very few of those I could offer as illustrations.

Example # 1: Berkshire Hathaway

Let's begin with Berkshire Hathaway and its Chairman Warren Buffett. In June of 1996, Buffett wrote a booklet for shareholders entitled *An Owner's Manual* in which he enumerated thirteen "owner-related" principles (shown here in italics). He later added commentary to each principle (the non-italicized portion). The first principle is:

> *Although our form is corporate, our attitude is partnership. Charlie Munger [Vice-Chairman] and I think of our shareholders as owner-partners, and of*

ourselves as managing partners.... We do not view the company itself as the ultimate owner of our business assets but instead view the company as a conduit through which our shareholders own the assets....

We think of Berkshire as being a non-managing partner in two extraordinary businesses, in which we measure our success by the long-term progress of the companies rather than by the month-to-month movements of their stocks. In fact, we would not care in the least if several years went by in which there was no trading, or quotation of prices, in the stocks of those companies. If we have good long-term expectations, short-term price changes are meaningless for us except to the extent they offer us an opportunity to increase our ownership at an attractive price.

This first principle says a great deal about operating any business. When executive leaders see themselves as partners with the shareholders, their perspective and basis for decision-making is fundamentally altered. We typically only enter into partnerships with others when we share long-term goals and objectives. This mindset insulates us from the frenetic knee-jerk reactions that result from leading a firm based upon daily stock price fluctuations.

His eighth principle states:

> A managerial "wish list" will not be filled at
> shareholder expense.... We will only do with your
> money what we would do with our own...

Sounds like a breath of fresh air after the executive abuses that have made headlines over the past year. But shouldn't all corporate executives and managers be expected to resist the temptation to enrich themselves inappropriately at the stockholders' expense? After all, are they not fiduciaries, bound by trust to care for the interests of others? Here again, the long-term versus short-term commitment of Berkshire Hathaway makes it much easier for executives to see their responsibility in the proper light.

Finally, principle number twelve:

> We will be candid in our reporting to you,
> emphasizing the pluses and minuses important in
> appraising business value. Our guideline is to tell you
> the business facts that we would want to know if our

positions were reversed. We owe you no less.
Moreover, as a company with a major
communications business, it would be inexcusable for
us to apply lesser standards of accuracy, balance and
incisiveness when reporting on ourselves than we would
expect our news people to apply when reporting on
others. We also believe candor benefits us as
managers: The CEO who misleads others in public
may eventually mislead himself in private.

At Berkshire you will find no "big bath"
accounting maneuvers or restructurings, nor any
"smoothing" of quarterly or annual results. We
will always tell you how many strokes we have
taken on each hole and never play around with
the scorecard.[xxiv]

Mr. Buffett's Principles frequently refer to what "we would
want...if our positions were reversed." Isn't this the Golden
Rule, "Do unto others as you would have them do unto
you"? I also appreciate his reference to the fact that lying
to others opens one up to self-deception. I have had the
sorry experience, on more than one occasion, of working
with senior executives in their fifties and sixties who, rather
than being at the peak of their careers, were burn-outs,

having become mere shadows of their former selves. Lying has a corrosive effect. Over time it eats away at our souls, until little remains of the vitality and inner strength we once possessed. In the end, we are caught in our own trap.

There is much to learn from Mr. Buffet's *Principles*, which reflect the underlying attitudes that have guided Berkshire Hathaway's success. For he and Vice-Chairman Charlie Munger, ethical compromise has not been necessary in order to achieve their business goals.

Example # 2: FedEx

FedEx has long been one of the most admired companies in the United States. From its support through the voluntary provision of transportation and logistics services for numerous charitable and philanthropic organizations such as the American Red Cross, America's Fund for Afghan Children and Heart to Heart International, to its direct support of the National Safe Kids Campaign and Orbis International's "flying eye hospital," FedEx clearly and consistently demonstrates its commitment to the global community.

The organization's values are clearly communicated through its Mission and Organization Statement.

> FedEx Corporation will produce superior financial returns for its shareholders by providing high value-added logistics, transportation and related information services through focused operating companies. Customer requirements will be met in the highest quality manner appropriate to each market segment served. FedEx Corporation will strive to develop mutually rewarding relationships with its employees, partners and suppliers. Safety will be the first consideration in all operations. Corporate activities will be conducted to the highest **ethical** and professional standards.
> *(Emphasis added by FedEx)*

FedEx, the worldwide leader in overnight package delivery believes that their activities must be "conducted to the highest **ethical** and professional standards." I believe that their reputation as one of the most highly regarded corporations in not only America, but the world, is a direct outgrowth of this commitment.

Example # 3: 3M

3M is another company that has a long-standing reputation for both excellent products and high ethical corporate behavior. This reputation was severely tested in the late 1990s, when it faced an ethical dilemma of immense proportions. One of 3M's leading products lines has been Scotchgard, which was used as a repellent for soil, water and oil on fabrics and carpeting; oil and grease resistant coatings in paper packaging; fire-fighting foams and other products. Scotchgard came into being in the 1950s, when a laboratory staff member spilled a compound on her shoe and was unable to remove it with water or solvents. It is this power to repel solids and liquids that made Scotchgard desirable; this and its persistence, the inability of other naturally occurring chemical compounds to break it down over time.

Some original Scotchgard formulations used as building blocks a fluorine based chemistry called perfluorooctanyl that repels other substances. Under certain conditions, materials from the chemistry could break down into a second related organic fluorine perfluorooctane sulfonate (PFOS) which is produced in both human and animal cells when specific precursor agents enter the cells. In the 1970s and

80s, 3M learned that the general population in the United States was registering very minute levels of organic fluorine in their blood serum, although experts had been unable to determine the specific form of fluorine or its source. Based upon this information, 3M began testing its workers for this organic compound and found it at slightly higher levels than in the general population. However, there appeared to be no health related problems stemming from these very low levels in both their workers and the general population.

In 1997, 3M tested worldwide samples of blood using a newly developed and much more sensitive regimen and found telltale traces of PFOS worldwide in both humans and animals, even in parts of the world that would likely have had no contact with Scotchgard or other similar chemistry products. Understanding the relationship between chemistry the company utilized and the PFOS present in blood serum, 3M began a program to test old blood samples taken prior to the introduction of Scotchgard. The result was clear, the old blood showed no signs of PFOS.

Following this discovery, 3M embarked upon an extensive testing and research program involving its own staff, outside experts, and the scientific community. It also began reporting its findings to the United States Environmental Protection Agency (EPA).

Although no data showed any detrimental health effects except at exposure levels many thousands of times higher than those found in either the 3M workers or the general public, 3M senior leadership made a landmark decision on May 16, 2000, that the company would phase-out the production of perfluorooctanyl chemistry over a two year period. This decision did not come without cost to 3M. At the time there were no known replacements for the chemistry used in many of the products by 3M, and numerous industrial customers were highly dependent upon the products. Sales from the affected product lines were $500 million annually, in addition to which 3M took a one-time charge of $200 million. 3M took this action voluntarily in spite of the fact that in the more than forty years of Scotchgard production, it had never been linked to any form of ailment. The leadership of 3M placed ethical behavior above profits.

Nevertheless, 3M did not rest on its laurels. The company redoubled its innovation and technological efforts in developing replacements for the discontinued chemistry. In 2002 alone, it will introduce eight new substitute Scotchgard product formulations that have very low toxicity and are unlikely to accumulate in humans or animals. 3M has received approval for commercialization of these new formulations from the EPA.[xxvi]

Example # 4: Midwest Express Airlines

Midwest Express began with the distinction of being the all "first class" airline and has maintained this unique model to the present day in both its airplane seating and in-flight meals, as well as its overall attitude toward customers. The airline's motto, "The best care in the air" applies equally to the way customers are treated on the ground.

Their mission statement includes the commitment "...to provide the highest quality travel experience to our customers...."[xxvii] They have repeatedly won the "best domestic airline" rating from both *Zagat* and *Conde Nast*, as well as similar awards from other organizations such as *Travel+Leisure*. Since the home of Midwest Express is Milwaukee, I have the benefit of enjoying their best care for most of my air travel requirements. Their emphasis on developing people has produced some remarkable results in an industry generally known for low morale among employees.

"First Class" Treatment

Observation # 1:

Part of Midwest's ability to turnaround aircraft quickly is due to the fact that, as soon as the passengers have deplaned, the entire crew, including pilot and co-pilot, clean the cabin.

Observation # 2:

On a recent flight, I noticed the captain assisting a young mother by carrying her baby in its infant carrier off the plane and up the jetway.

Observation # 3:

On one of my last-minute trips to Washington, D.C., I arrived at the gate late to find the jetway already rolled back from the plane. After I explained the urgency of my mission to the gate attendant, she called the pilot, who directed that the jetway be extended and the aircraft door reopened so that I could board.

Conclusion:

An organization that seriously and consistently invests into its people instills in them an ethic to help others, which in turn pays huge dividends for the corporation.

Example # 4: Wendy's International

Dave Thomas, the founder of Wendy's, provided a powerful reminder of what "a common guy," as he frequently referred to himself, can accomplish. Dave began life as an unlikely candidate for success. He was born in Atlantic City, N.J. in 1932 to an unwed mother who he would never have the opportunity to meet before she died eighteen years later. However, Dave was one of the "lucky" babies; he was adopted by a couple in Michigan, though his adoptive mother died when he was five and life thereafter was anything but ideal.

In his book *Well Done! The Common Guy's Guide to Everyday Success*, Dave shared his "Twelve Ingredients of Success." These he grouped into four categories.

DAVE THOMAS' TWELVE INGREDIENTS OF SUCCESS

INWARD	**OUTWARD**
getting your act together	*treating people right*
Honesty	Caring
Faith	Teamwork
Discipline	Support
UPWARD	**ONWARD**
going for excellence and beyond	*putting yourself second and others first*
Motivation	Responsibility
Creativity	Courage
Leadership	Generosity

Dave Thomas demonstrated all of these attributes in his role as Wendy's Senior Chairman as well as in his personal life. I find it interesting to note that during the six-month period of January through June 2002, while the S&P 500 dropped 15% in value, Wendy's stock rose 30%. Is it possible that investors have already begun to search out those companies with high ethical principles?[xxviii]

Actions *speak louder than* Words

In 1990, Dave led the Wendy's corporation into a very public two-year leadership campaign for the cause of adoption. Then, in 1992, he founded the Dave Thomas Foundation for Adoption. The foundation serves as an active voice for over 150,000 children in North America's public child welfare system who live in shelters and foster homes. These are children who are older, belong to sibling groups that desire to be adopted together, are from minority and mixed cultures or who are physically or mentally challenged. The foundation's vision is simple, that "Every child will have a permanent and loving home."

In his book *Well Done!* Dave quotes Nan Keohane, President of Duke University in saying, "If you hedge the truth yourself, it's hard to persuade others that you mean what you say when you ask for honesty from them."[xxix]   Dave Thomas built Wendy's into an $8.3 billion company by emphasizing his core values. Interestingly, a smiling photo on the back cover of the book shows him, the Senior Chairman, wearing a Wendy's apron, with one hand on a mop and the other on a bucket handle. Dave Thomas was an outstanding example of success by virtue of transparent integrity as a true servant leader.

Example # 5: ServiceMaster

ServiceMaster is very unique as a public company in that its senior executives have made no secret of their leadership style and objectives, although these are highly unusual. The company expresses its philosophy by way of the following four objectives:

Objective One: To honor God in all we do

> We believe that every person — regardless of personal beliefs or differences — has been created in the image and likeness of God. We seek to recognize the

dignity, worth and potential of each individual and believe that everyone has intrinsic worth and value. This objective challenges us to have commitment to truth and to deliver what we promise. It provides the basis for our belief in servant leadership. It is not an expression of a particular religious belief, or a basis for exclusion. Rather, it is a mandate for inclusion, and a constant reminder for us to do the right thing in the right way.

Objective Two: To help people develop

At ServiceMaster, work is about developing, contributing and feeling the accomplishment of a job well done. ServiceMaster believes in not only empowering people, but also enabling them to succeed. By giving people the tools and training to develop, we increase their productivity and earnings, and enhance the dignity, self-respect and worth of each individual.

Objective Three: To pursue excellence

We continually seek better methods of delivering service and believe that every time we touch a customer's life, we should provide added value for that customer. Pursuing excellence means that we must know our customers, understand their needs and expectations, regularly listen to them and adjust our processes and procedures to more effectively serve them.

Objective Four: **To grow profitably**

By achieving economic success, we will have the resources to positively affect the lives of our shareholders, customers and associates.
Profitability is a way to test and challenge us. Profitability, productivity and quality reflect added value for our customers, a fair return for our shareholders, and improved opportunity for our people.[xxx]

ServiceMaster has a long reputation of doing just that. The company services 10.5 million residential customers each year. In addition, it also provides service to the commercial and international markets. It accomplishes this through its network of 5,400 company owned and franchised service centers and business units.

Bad Things *happen to* Good People

Despite admirable objectives, ServiceMaster, in particular

its Terminix operations, has experienced some legal problems based upon customer accusations of poor quality, bad faith and even fraud. I believe that this is important to note, because no matter how laudable the intentions and conduct of an organization's executive leadership may be, this cannot guarantee immunity from the inappropriate conduct of subordinates. Bad things can still happen.

ServiceMaster's vast operations network, including its franchisees, open it, like any other corporation, to the unscrupulous actions of a few renegades who can compromise the entire organization's reputation. Despite ServiceMaster's best efforts at policing all of its employees and franchisees, no amount of oversight can prevent every unauthorized act.

While unfortunate, such breaches should not lessen our resolve to develop character-based organizations. Vigilant leadership must constantly be on guard for those within the corporation willing to compromise the organization's standards for personal gain. It is important to recognize that when we empower people to act independently, we must accept the risk and potential for wrongdoing.

Such occurrences need not ruin an otherwise exemplary

reputation, such as that of ServiceMaster, as long as executive leaders act decisively to isolate and stop those who are responsible and simultaneously apply their example as a learning experience for the rest of the organization. A clear demonstration of the corporation's absolute intolerance of unethical behavior can serve as a strong deterrent to others. Although it can be greatly discouraging to have years of consistent ethical behavior suddenly overshadowed by the widely publicized dishonesty of a few, it is incumbent on leaders to follow ServiceMaster's example in not seeking the easy way out, either by attempting to cover-up wrong-doing or faltering in their pursuit of ethical excellence.

The Antidote...

Our problem is not that we *must* bend the ethical rules in order to be prosperous, but rather that too many executives *believe* that they must, and this misperception becomes their distorted reality. The fact is that high ethical standards do not destroy an organization's ability to carry on business and prosper; standards instead promote sustainable growth and provide the strongest long-term protection for the organization's future.

The history of this great nation was forever changed by one man—one man with vision and the courage to carry that vision to its end.

~ JOHN DI FRANCES

CHAPTER FOUR
[chapter]

IV

VISIONARY LEADERSHIP
CAN TURN THE TIDE
AN EXAMPLE FROM HISTORY

CHAPTER FOUR

History offers many object lessons confirming the crucial value of claiming and holding the high ground in warfare, as well as documenting the vision, courage and commitment required to do so. However, few are clearer than that of General John Buford at the Battle of Gettysburg.

On the sultry, final day of June 1863, the Army of the South, 70,000 plus strong, under the command of the peerless General Robert E. Lee, wound its way into the northern state of Pennsylvania. It seemed as though a vast swarm of gray locusts had emerged, pouring down through the passes to the west and north of the Blue Ridge Mountains. That summer had been unbearably hot and dry. As the vast Confederate army emerged from the green mountains, a column of dust rose high above it, silently marking its steady advance.

Meanwhile, a lead element of the Union Cavalry consisting of only two brigades, a total of 2,500 men, under the command of Brigadier General John Buford moved toward Gettysburg. Buford, a West Point graduate and experienced soldier, was still recovering from wounds received at the Second Battle of Bull Run ten months earlier.

Upon approaching Gettysburg, Buford surveyed the scene before him from a hilltop cemetery. When he noticed Confederate troops scurrying about from building to building, his first reaction was to assume that this was merely a rebel raiding party scouring the countryside for supplies. However, as he gazed through field glasses up the Cashtown Road, past the red brick seminary and into the hills beyond, he could see that a sizable force of troops was moving down the Chambersburg Road toward the town and his position. He began to sense the power behind this force still hidden in the lush green vegetation of the mountains beyond. If his appraisal was correct, the whole

Rebel army was moving his way, instead of toward Harrisburg, as the Union High Command believed.

Upon discovering a line of Union blue cavalry in the hills to the south of town, the Confederate soldiers began slowly retreating, back through Gettysburg's streets, past the seminary and eventually up the road in the direction from which they had come. It was clear to Buford that, without the aid of their cavalry and reliable information about the force that lay before them, the rebel troops had been ordered not to begin a fight.

He could see it all clearly...
as if it were already happening

Buford assembled his staff and informed them of his firm belief that the whole of Lee's army would be coming down that road the following morning, right through town and onto the heights beyond. From there, the Confederates would easily rain down fire upon General Meade, the Union Commander, and his army when they finally arrived. As a seasoned commander, Buford could see it all clearly, as clearly as if it were already happening. It would be just like the other battles thus far in the war: Lee and his army on the high ground and Meade with his blue-clad Union boys attempting to charge across a withering mile or more field of fire.

Another Northern defeat seemed inevitable—and there was nothing to stop it. Buford anticipated Meade's army straggling into Gettysburg around midday on July 1st, at the earliest. By then, the Confederates would have placed enough divisions on the heights above town to deny the high ground to the Union. The result would be another slaughter when Northern troops charged valiantly in wave after wave against the entrenched Confederates, just as they had done so many times before.

There was, however, one hope. The Rebel columns had to descend down the narrow Chambersburg Road and, if they could be delayed, stacked up on the road before they broke out into the open at Gettysburg; the delay might last just long enough to allow Meade's advance units to arrive first and secure the high ground. Buford thought the plan just might work, but to delay the Confederate Army meant that his own two brigades would have to hold off the Rebel assaults alone for several hours. There was a possibility that it could be done.

In fact, Buford's own men had done it at the Second Battle

of Manassas (Bull Run) where Buford had been wounded. There, with 2,500 cavalry, they had held out against General Longstreet's superior force of 30,000, but the Union General Pope had never come to their relief. Pope had dismissed reports of Longstreet's presence and strength.

Major General Fitz-John Porter had been in command there at Thorofare Gap, and for his efforts had been drummed out of the Northern army by Pope. It did not pay to be a failed hero in the Union army, especially when a senior commander felt the need for a scapegoat. What if Buford tried to hold again, this time with Lee's whole 70,000 man army coming down the road? And what if Meade's army did not arrive in time?

A Man of Character...

Then again, the lead unit of the Union army was that of Major General John Reynolds. Reynolds was a man of character, a good and honorable man. In fact, there was a time when he had been offered command of the Union army, and many wished he had taken it. He had said, however, privately, that there was too much interference from the War Department in Washington. They would not allow their commanders the flexibility to fight this war, and for this reason he had declined the position. So now the Union troops were stuck with Meade, cautious, careful and s-l-o-w Meade.

Buford's mind was already made up. For better or worse, the calvary would stand and they would hold. They would pray that Reynolds heeded Buford's message and came in time, but they would hold! With his decision firmly made, Buford turned his attention to the tasks at hand, first setting his men along the roads west and north of Gettysburg. He then sat down to compose a message to General Reynolds' upon whose action the outcome of this great endeavor would rest. About midnight, the courier returned after delivering his message. Reynolds was pleased with the news and promised to come in the morning as early as possible.

Now, let us return briefly to the present. Why are we comparing the decisions of a Civil War general with the conduct of modern day executives? What's the connection? John Buford understood leadership. He recognized the importance of claiming the high ground, having the foresight to understand its value—that its control would likely decide the battle. Buford took decisive action fully aware of the risks involved. He knew what was at stake and what must be done, committed to it and did not look back. The following is the account of what took place.

He knew what was at stake and what must be done, committed to it and did not look back.

Soon after dawn, the Confederate troops began to move. They were wasting no time. Buford knew that, at best, his men could not hold out long. They would force the enemy's lead element to deploy, thus jamming up the road and preventing the remainder of the column from advancing.

And the pressure came...

But once the Rebels deployed, Buford's men would come under enormous pressure. They were strung out single-file along the two roads, one man every three feet. The Confederates, once in formation, would be shoulder-to-shoulder, rank upon rank. They would be exposed; Buford's men were dug in. Together with their new repeating carbine rifles, this was their only advantage—this and whatever brief element of surprise they might initially enjoy, but it would certainly be gone within the opening minutes of battle.

Buford did not have long to wait until the stillness of early morning was shattered by warning shots fired by his pickets at the bridge, closely followed by the thunder of his own cannon. Within moments came the small arms fire, first from his men and then the return volleys of the enemy. The first skirmish was short lived. The Rebels recoiled, and all was quiet again.

They know we are here now, thought Buford. *Probably think it is just the cavalry patrol from yesterday. They will be back shortly to test our strength.* He was right. They came again before long, still not in any strength, probing to find out what was ahead of them. This time the fight lasted longer and was more intense. The Confederate advance was still disorganized, however, not a coordinated attack. When it was over, Buford's men were still holding strong.

Buford was pleased, but he knew the next attack would be in earnest. Back they came—and this time the roar of battle was clear. Buford's cannon could now be heard as the battle raged on up and down the west road for some time. Finally, it ended. Once again, Buford's lines held, and the enemy fell back. By now, however, casualties were steadily mounting. The already razor-thin Union lines were being stretched even more. Still, there was no sign of Reynolds.

Buford, learning that his brigade to the north had not seen any action yet, sent a message to transfer all possible troops from there to the western line of defense. This served both to fill in some of the now empty gaps in the line where men had fallen and to lengthen the lines in order to reduce the risk of being flanked.

Then the sounds of battle began again. Buford looked through his field glasses. The noise grew much louder; now, in addition to the volleying of his own small cannon, he heard the larger Confederate cannon open up. This was a major, coordinated attack. The end was coming. His fifteen hundred or so remaining men on the line were now facing a Confederate force of close to 10,000. Buford knew they could not hold out much longer. The Rebel cannon were beginning to take their toll.

Even if his dismounted cavalry remained in place, they would soon be overrun by successive waves of infantry. The line began to give way in several places, but each time men filled in to repulse their attackers. Finally, the rebel infantry broke and began to retreat, but only to regroup for another, more massive attack.

Buford ascended the cupola of the seminary where his

signal crew had established a lookout post, both to monitor the battle and to watch for Reynolds' reinforcements. From there he checked his battered lines and then turned his attention south to look in earnest for General Reynolds' infantry.

Just when Buford was about to give up hope, he saw, on the Taneytown Road to the south, a telltale wisp of dust rising above the trees—mounted soldiers, clad in blue, but not cavalry. Reynolds and his aids were now riding fast, but no infantry was in sight behind them. As the mounted party arrived at the seminary, Reynolds called up to Buford, "What's the matter John?" To this Buford replied, "The devil's to pay!"

By now Buford could see Reynolds' men on the double quick surging down the road and breaking out across the fields in a shortcut to the battle line where his own vastly outnumbered men were desperately hanging on. It was now about 10:00 in the morning of July 1, 1863, and General Reynolds' troops had already covered the eight miles to Gettysburg in the sweltering heat.

Reynold's reinforcements quickly began filling in the ranks between Buford's men. Reynolds congratulated Buford on the job he had done—his two brigades had kept the whole of Lee's army bottled up for nearly four hours. In so doing, he had preserved the heights for Meade's forces. For the first time, the Union army would have the tactical advantage, and General Lee would be forced to attack in a deadly charge across open fields that lay before the high ground.

The battle that day was far from over; it would, in fact, last another six and a half hours. Reynolds' troops were just beginning to approach the then mile-wide line of battle while the Confederate troops were already deployed in significant strength. The Confederates would, through the course of the day, drive the arriving Union troops down the road and back through Gettysburg. Although Buford's cavalry initially began the day with the advantage of position, the numerically superior Southern force of fifteen to twenty thousand men deployed would eventually overmatch the Union's eight thousand infantry troops that had arrived in time for the day's fighting. However, as dusk settled, the Union columns behind Reynolds' I Corps would be moving onto the heights and digging in for the decisive battles of July 2nd and 3rd.

Reynolds dispatched a message to General Meade that

their line had held and that the ground Buford had chosen was good ground for the coming fight. He then ordered Buford to withdraw his cavalry to regroup and refit. They had been hit hard, but they stood fast. They had never given in. They had held the day.

That afternoon, unaware of the efficacy of Buford's actions in preserving the high ground for the Union, General Hancock had mentioned to General Howard, "... I think this the strongest position by nature upon which to fight a battle that I ever saw...." It would still be some time before headquarters learned of the valiant and strategic interruption of Lee's advance by Buford's cavalry. The Union successes on July 2nd and 3rd were directly due to the actions of Buford and his men on July 1st in Reclaiming the High Ground.

One Man Changed the Future

Despite General Meade's failure to counter-attack following Pickett's failed charge on July 3rd and to pursue Lee's battered and fleeing army on July 4th, Union control of the high ground at Gettysburg had turned the tide of the war. Because Meade had foolishly allowed Lee's army to slip away across the Potomac, the war would rage on for two more years. However, Buford's foresight undeniably altered the outcome of the Civil War.[xxxi]

The history of this great nation was forever changed by one man—one man with vision and the courage to carry that vision to its end. Today we face different battles. As the free enterprise system comes under attack from both external and internal foes, we too must reclaim the high ground and fight for the core values that have long allowed this system to flourish.

A reclaiming of the ethical high ground is the only course at hand that will once again return the public and the investor community's trust in corporate America. Greed, selfishness and deception, the antithesis of good character, are the enemy of a free economic system. Clearly, we have large gaps in our lines of defense. The dot com insanity of the 1990s fueled a small-scale market collapse. This was an unheeded early warning of the havoc we are now experiencing. Unless we act to restore high ethical standards to corporate business, a continuation of the growing trust deficit will inevitably lead to even greater collapses of our capital markets.

An honorable legacy cannot be built overnight—
it takes years. And sooner or later, it requires
decisions rooted deeply in high ethical character.

~ JOHN DI FRANCES

CHAPTER FIVE
[chapter]

LEADERS MUST MAKE
THE DIFFERENCE

CHAPTER FIVE

The prescription is simple: develop organizations of high ethical character. In this context, we define character as personal integrity in doing what is right regardless of circumstances or possible cost. It requires leadership with vision and courage. The implementation is straightforward: an organization's leaders must first clearly set the standards for all to know and then model them for all to see. It's that simple, and also that difficult.

Setting high ethical standards will require some serious soul-searching on the part of the organization's leadership.

This is not an issue that can be addressed by adopting a "canned" approach or program. In fact, that has been the problem with most of the so-called "Ethics Programs" attempted by both corporations and government agencies. The development of such band-aid approaches has been delegated down to a perfunctory level in the organization, where typically a mid-level or lower manager has been given an office with "Ethics Officer" inscribed on the doorplate. Soon forgotten, out of the way of everyone doing any serious work in the organization, the office and officer function much like the lonely Maytag repairman on old television commercials, unknown, unwanted and totally ineffective.

The CEO *must be the* Corporate Conscience.

The CEO must not only be actively engaged in the function of Chief Executive Officer, but just as crucially in that of Chief Ethics Officer and corporate conscience of the organization. In this manner, the ethical standards of the organization will be apparent from the top down in every discussion, decision and action.

Modeling the organization's ethical standard will require a daily commitment to doing what is right when others are watching as well as when no one else is around to notice. The standard must become more important than the outcome and the code of conduct a measure of individual accountability.

The Standard *must be more* Important

To be outcome driven is not bad in itself. The problem lies in our perception of what that outcome should be. Remember Harvey Firestone and the reference to his confidence "that in the long run, right will ultimately prevail, he faced difficulty unafraid, taking long views of life" as well as Emerson's statement, "to believe what the centuries say against the years and the hours."[xxxii] Vision is an essential attribute for leadership. It enables leaders to see not only the present, obvious circumstances the organization faces, but also to see beyond, well into the future.

Corporate leaders need to recognize and appreciate the fact that their present day actions will outlive the immediate financial results. When the day is done, we all leave a legacy. It is a legacy of honor or dishonor. This is a principle that Firestone, Enron, Andersen, Global Crossing, Merrill Lynch, Qwest, Worldcom and a myriad of others are just beginning to realize while company after company restates its past several years' earnings.

When, in 1982, a few bottles of Johnson & Johnson's Tylenol capsules were found to be laced with cyanide, the company faced two choices. The seemingly expedient choice for the short-term was to hunker-down, say nothing, attempt to cover it up, and quietly pay off the few families affected. They could then use their media power to vilify the criminal responsible for the deaths, thereby shifting attention away from the company. Instead, Johnson & Johnson chose to face the crisis head-on. They immediately informed the government and press of the product tampering and proceeded to recall in excess of $100 million worth of product to ensure that no further danger would be posed to the public. Corporate earnings and stock price were both negatively impacted. Some commentators thought the total recall decision would spell the end of the Tylenol brand.

The following year Johnson & Johnson was ranked in the top three most admired companies and has continued to consistently remain highly regarded by the public. Meanwhile, the Tylenol brand has not only survived, but has expanded to other products, with Johnson & Johnson emerging from the crisis as the pioneer of tamper proof packaging, a new industry in itself.

An **Honorable Legacy** *takes* **Years** *to build.*

An honorable legacy cannot be built overnight—it takes years. And sooner or later, it requires decisions rooted deeply in high ethical character. For General John Buford, reclaiming the high ground came at a great cost. He tenaciously held under fire until help finally came. He had to stand firm in order to achieve the goal. So also, CEO's and other corporate leaders must stand firm, resisting siege-like pressures from investors and analysts alike, who demand ever greater earnings today with no understanding of the enormous costs that a future implosion of trust will generate.

However great the struggle, corporate leaders who do stand firm will reap peace of mind as their first reward. They need not fear any "goblins" lurking in the corporate closet. There will be nothing to hide. Standing firm is the price to be paid for a good name, and, when weighed over the long term, a good name will build the trust and credibility by which a corporation and its leaders will inevitably be judged.

Lead by Daily Example

This leadership responsibility is not a function that can be delegated away. We have witnessed too many senior executives who, after the fact, claim to have been totally ignorant of the fraudulent activity underlying their company's profits as well as the enormous financial rewards they have personally received. The duty to lead by daily example in the course of common events and activities is crucial to instilling and enforcing the ethical standards of an organization. Without such leadership in action, the standards become nothing more than hollow rhetoric.

Where do leaders come from? Are they simply a haphazard assortment of brains and personality? Or rather, is good leadership the result of careful and continuous training deliberately focused on the development of knowledge, thinking skills, positive attitudes and high ethics?

How are leaders trained? Ideally, it begins in early childhood by loving parents who clearly understand, model and teach good character. This emphasis on instilling moral virtue should then be reinforced throughout childhood and adolescence by churches, schools and the community at large.

And what of the training our future business leaders receive as adults? Are the B-schools on top of this critical issue and incorporating the development of high ethical character into their curriculum for enterprising MBA students destined to become the future leaders of many of our largest corporations? Sadly, the answer is very often, no. Although a few B-schools do recognize the growing need for ethics training and place a significant emphasis on ethics, most do not. Unfortunately, ethics training is seldom given serious consideration by academia, and is most often reduced to a single ethics course or disregarded all together. A recent *BusinessWeek* article on the subject stated:

> ...adding a strong ethics component to the B-school culture will be no sure thing. After all, it's a fine line that schools must walk: MBA programs pack into two very expensive years a lifetime's worth of functional tools for graduates, who see their primary role as making money for shareholders and themselves—and not necessarily in that order.

> Other common excuses at the nation's B-schools include "We're too busy teaching our core material," or, "MBA students are grown people—we can't teach them ethics."[xxxiii]

Educating the "Huns"

"A lifetime's worth of functional tools?" "Too busy teaching core material?" Could any subject be more central to the lifetime functioning of a business executive than ethics? Of what value is the ability to perform analysis without the ethical basis upon which to make moral decisions based upon the analysis? Are we simply educating the "Huns" into being more efficient butchers? And as for the argument that we cannot teach grown adults ethics, it is a sad commentary that we must begin the process at this point in their lives. Yet, if that is truly the case, then begin at adulthood we must.

How can it be that an ethics curriculum has no place in our B-schools where grown men and women are taught how to win the battles of business? However, by necessity, ethics courses and the importance of an ethical lifestyle are considered indispensable to the training required for those who will lead our nation on the battlefields of real wars around the globe. Would anyone want our military leaders to function in an ethical and moral vacuum? I think not.

On the 27th of January, 2000, the former Commandant of the United States Marine Corps, General Charles Krulak gave the following speech to the Joint Services Conference on Professional Ethics (JSCOPE).

We study and discuss ethical principles because it serves to strengthen and validate our own inner value system...it gives direction to what I call our own moral compass. It is the understanding of ethics that becomes the foundation upon which we can deliberately commit to inviolate principles. It becomes the basis of what we are... of what we include in our character. Based on it, we commit to doing what is right. We expect such commitment from our leaders, but most importantly, we must demand it from ourselves.

Sound morals and ethical behavior cannot be established or created in a day...a semester...or a year. They must be institutionalized within our character over time...they must become a way of life. They go beyond our individual [military] services and beyond our ranks and positions. They cut to the heart and to the soul of who we are and what we are and what we must be...men and women of character. They arm us for the challenges to come and they impart to us a sense of wholeness. They unite us in the calling we now know as the profession of arms.

Of all the moral and ethical guideposts that we have been brought up to recognize, the one that, for me, stands above the rest... the one that I have kept in the forefront of my mind...is integrity. It is my ethical and personal touchstone.

Integrity as we know it today, stands for soundness of moral principle and character—uprightness—honesty. Yet there is more. Integrity is also an ideal...a goal to strive for...and for a man or woman to "walk in their integrity" is to require constant discipline and usage. The word integrity itself is a martial word that comes to us from an ancient Roman army tradition.

During the time of the twelve Caesars, the Roman army would conduct morning inspections. As the inspecting Centurion would come in front of each legionnaire, the soldier would strike with his right fist the armor breastplate that covered his heart. The armor had to be strongest there in order to protect the heart from the sword thrusts and from arrow strikes. As the soldier struck his armor, he would shout "integritas" [in-teg-ri-tas], which in Latin means material wholeness, completeness and entirety. The inspecting Centurion would listen closely for this affirmation and also for the ring that well kept armor would give off. Satisfied that the armor was sound and that the soldier beneath it was protected, he would then move on to the next man.

At about the same time, the Praetorians or imperial bodyguard were ascending into power and influence; drawn from the best "politically correct" soldiers of the legions, they received the finest equipment and armor. They no longer had to shout "integritas" to signify that their armor was sound. Instead, as they struck their breastplate, they would shout "Hail Caesar," to signify that their heart belonged to the imperial personage—not to their unit—not to an institution—not to a code of ideals. They armored themselves to serve the cause of a single man.

A century passed and the rift between the legion and the imperial bodyguard and its excesses grew larger. To signify the difference between the two organizations, the legionnaire, upon striking his armor would no longer shout "integritas," but instead would shout "integer" [in-te-ger].

Integer means undiminished—complete—perfect.
It not only indicated that the armor was sound, it
also indicated that the soldier wearing the armor
was sound of character. He was complete in his
integrity...his heart was in the right place...his
standards and morals were high. He was not
associated with the immoral conduct that was
rapidly becoming the signature of the Praetorian
Guards.

The armor of integrity continued to serve the
legion well. For over four centuries they held the
line against the marauding Goths and Vandals,
but by 383 A.D., the social decline that infected
the republic and the Praetorian Guard had its
effects upon the legion.

As a 4th century Roman general wrote, "When
because of negligence and laziness, parade ground
drills were abandoned, the customary armor
began to feel heavy since the soldiers rarely, if
ever, wore it. Therefore, they first asked the
emperor to set aside the breastplates and mail

and then the helmets. So our soldiers fought the Goths without any protection for the heart and head and were often beaten by archers. Although there were many disasters, which led to the loss of great cities, no one tried to restore the armor to the infantry. They took their armor off and when the armor came off—so too came their integrity." It was only a matter of a few years until the legion rotted from within and was unable to hold the frontiers. The barbarians were at the gates.

Integrity...is a combination of the words, integritas and integer. It refers to the putting on of armor, of building a completeness...a wholeness...a wholeness in character. How appropriate that the word integrity is a derivative of two words describing the character of a member of the profession of arms.

The military has a tradition of producing great leaders that possess the highest ethical standards and integrity. It produces men and women of character...character that allows them to deal ethically with the challenges of today and to make conscious decisions about how they will approach tomorrow. However, as I mentioned earlier, this is not done instantly. It requires that integrity becomes a way of life...it must be woven into the very fabric of our soul. Just as was true in the days of imperial Rome, you either walk in your integrity daily, or you take off the armor of the "integer" and leave your heart and soul exposed...open to attack.

My challenge to you is simple, but often very difficult...wear your armor of integrity...take full measure of its weight...find comfort in its protection. Do not become lax. And always, always, remember that no one can take your integrity from you...you and only you can give it away!

The Biblical book of practical ethics—better known as the book of Proverbs—sums it up very nicely, "The integrity of the upright shall guide them: but the perverseness of transgressors shall destroy them." (Proverbs 11:3)[xxxiv]

Our military academies have not forgotten the importance of instilling ethics in their students. Why have our B-schools?

"You either walk in your integrity daily, or you...leave your heart and soul exposed...open to attack."

I can recall a number of occasions when I was asked to advise troubled corporations which, interestingly enough, displayed plaques on their reception area walls proclaiming a commitment to quality assurance programs and customer service initiatives. Paradoxically, these plaques announced company programs and policies that, if truly followed, would have made my presence unnecessary.

On one occasion, a defense contractor whose office displayed a framed set of such documents retained me. One of these plaques was the company's ISO 9000 Quality Registration and the other was a "Commitment to Quality First" signed by the firm's CEO. I was asked to review a contract in which they were experiencing problems meeting the performance criteria for a U.S. military grenade component for troops. It soon became clear to me that the production run was noncompliant with the contract specifications. When I stated my findings and the appropriate solution, I was told that this remedy was too costly and that the company's intention was, instead, to falsify the product inspection and certification records. In addition to explaining the legal civil and criminal ramifications of such actions, I also pointed out the clear ethical and moral contradiction this represented, given the statements of quality exhibited in the reception area. To my chagrin, I was informed by the Vice President of Manufacturing that the documents on display were intended to create a "positive impression" on visiting customers. I notified the CEO, who had retained my firm, of my disgust and departed immediately. It is clear that the rhetoric in that organization was just that—rhetoric.

In 1977, I joined an independent petroleum company. Over the next six years, I rose rapidly through the company and was responsible for a wide scope of operations as well as a strategic initiative for new business opportunities. However, in 1983, I became concerned about one particular aspect of the company and repeatedly expressed my sentiments. One day at a senior management meeting, I concluded that not only would the behavior that concerned me continue, but it was certain to escalate. Later that afternoon, I went to the president of the company, to whom I reported, and once again voiced my strong concern; I told him that I had decided to resign because of the ethical implications. He assured me that the problem would be resolved and asked me to remain with the company. When I told him that I could not in good conscience remain, he asked me to at least think about it overnight.

That evening I discussed the issues with my wife, and shared my belief that it would be dishonest for me to remain when my conscience dictated otherwise. She agreed that I should resign immediately, not only to distance myself from the improper activities, but also to make a statement to the rest of the management team. The following morning I resigned.

"Ethically, I had no choice but to distance myself from the behavior that I believed to be improper."

This was not a practical decision from a financial standpoint. I had a good position with work I enjoyed. My wife was within two weeks of delivering our third child, and as I had not been contemplating an employment change, I had no immediate prospects or even a current resume. In addition, there were personal family considerations that precluded my accepting opportunities that required relocation.

Although the circumstances appeared bleak, the decision to resign was easy to reach. Ethically, I had no choice but to distance myself from the behavior that I believed to be improper. A year and a half later, the company collapsed due directly to the continuation of the activities I had stood against. Despite the fact that the financial consequences were for a number of years severe, I have been thankful ever since that I took the action I did, because my name was not in any way associated with the company's ultimate bankruptcy and liquidation. Meanwhile, although unplanned on my part, departure from the company would open the door for me to begin my own firm.

One of the hallmarks of ethical leadership is a strong emphasis on relationships. This is borne out in many ways, one of which is mentoring. In so doing, senior executives make a lasting investment in the lives of rising leaders, being held mutually accountable and guiding by good example.

The Test...

Accountability is the test of true commitment to immutable standards. When we pass that test on a continuing daily basis, those we lead will take our standards seriously.

First, we must remember the high standards that come with high office.

~ PRESIDENT GEORGE W. BUSH

CHAPTER SIX

[chapter]

VI

RAISING THE STANDARD

CHAPTER SIX

W hen President George W. Bush took office, one of his first official acts on January 20, 2001, was to issue a "Memorandum for the Heads of Executive Departments and Agencies of the United States Government." The purpose of this memorandum was to establish Standards of Conduct as, "Everyone who enters into public service for the United States has a duty to the American people to maintain the highest standards of integrity in Government."[xxxv]

In so doing the President commented:

> First, we must remember the high standards that
> come with high office. This begins with careful
> adherence to the rules. I expect every member of
> this administration to stay well within the boundaries
> that define legal and ethical conduct. This means
> avoiding even the appearance of problems. This
> means checking and, if need be, double-checking
> that the rules have been obeyed. This means never
> compromising those rules.[xxxv]

The President made no exceptions, not even for himself.
"No one in the White House should be afraid to confront
the people they work for, for ethical concerns. And no one
should hesitate to confront me, as well. We're all accountable
to one another. And above all, we're all accountable to the
law and to the American people."

Promises Made...Promises Kept

President Bush made it perfectly clear that his intent is to
"restore honor and integrity" to the presidency. "I want it
said of us that promises made were promises kept."

I had the privilege recently of being invited to speak at the grand opening of AAL (Aid Association of Lutherans) Bank & Trust. During the reception beforehand, I noticed several copies of a coffee-table book placed around the bank lobby. It had recently been printed in commemoration of AAL's one-hundredth anniversary. The book, which traced the humble beginnings of the organization to its merger in 2002 with Lutheran Brotherhood, was aptly titled *Promises Kept*. What a stark contrast to the Enron legacy!

In keeping with the President's Standards of Official Conduct for federal government organizations, I have taken the liberty of modifying these for application to the corporate world. This is in no way intended to provide "the solution" to the present problem. It is rather intended only as a beginning point from which leaders of corporate organizations may launch their own soul searching efforts in *Reclaiming the Ethical High Ground by Developing Organizations of Character*.

CORPORATE CONDUCT
establishing the code

1. Corporate service is a trust, requiring employees at all levels of the organization to place ethical principles above monetary and status gains.

2. No employee shall act in such a manner as to place their personal financial interests above the conscientious performance of their duty.

3. Employees shall not engage in financial transactions using nonpublic corporate information or allow the improper use of such information to further any private or competing interest.

4. An employee shall not, except as permitted by company policy, solicit or accept any significant gift or other item or service of monetary value from any person or entity seeking to or doing business with or whose interests may be substantially affected by the performance or nonperformance of the employee's duties.

5. All employees shall put forth full and honest effort in the performance of their duties.

6. Employees shall not knowingly make unauthorized commitments or promises of any kind purporting to bind the company.

7. Employees shall not use their position improperly for private gain.

8. Employees shall act impartially and not give preferential treatment to any private organization or individual.

9. Employees shall protect and conserve the company's property, both physical and intellectual, and shall not use it for unauthorized activities.

10. Employees shall not engage in outside employment or activities, including seeking or negotiating for employment, in any manner that conflicts with their official duties and responsibilities to the company.

11. Employees shall disclose waste, fraud, abuse, and corruption to appropriate authorities, without fear of retribution by the corporation or any individuals within the organization for any legitimate disclosure.

12. Employees shall endeavor to avoid any actions creating even the appearance that they are violating applicable law or the ethical standards of this code of conduct.

Companies that follow a strict ethical code will find it easier to both recruit and retain employees, from entry level to CEOs. Gerald R. Roche, the Senior Chairman of Heidrick & Struggles, a top executive search firm states, "The No. 1

criteria in every CEO search we do today is integrity. That used to be assumed. No one had to mention it. Not anymore."[xxxvi]

Nor is it only companies that are becoming more particular. Potential CEOs themselves are now very concerned about the reputation, accounting practices and business ethics of potential employers who approach them. There have lately been numerous instances of major corporations that have been turned down repeatedly by CEO candidates, leaving top level executive positions vacant. The *Wall Street Journal*, in an article entitled "Fearing Scandals, Executives Spurn CEO Job Offers" quoted W. James McNerney, who accepted the top position at 3M after rejecting other offers as saying, "I knew this would be a big decision and that wherever I went there would be risks. I chose 3M because it's a business I understand with good people and great integrity...I knew what I was getting into."[xxxvii]

Some prospective CEOs have become so concerned about the reputation of companies as to retain due-diligence consultants to verify information provided by the corporation. Many have also taken to conducting in-depth interviews of board members to ascertain their true level of governance oversight.

Employers who model good character and are careful to maintain this standard among employees create an extremely positive work environment for everyone. This fosters a community where people feel they are valued and appreciated, receiving support and respect from their fellow workers. Such an environment encourages open communication and higher productivity as well as improving long term employee retention, thereby reducing training and turnover costs. In short, the workplace becomes a place to grow, to interact and to make a significant contribution.

Ultimately, when it comes to developing an organization of character, what leaders say, how they act, and whom they esteem must reflect a consistent message of honor, integrity and high ethical character.

~ JOHN DI FRANCES

CHAPTER SEVEN

[chapter]

VII

KEYS TO MAINTAINING
HIGH ETHICAL STANDARDS

CHAPTER SEVEN

What It Takes to Create an Organization of Character

No magic formula exists for transforming your organization into a paragon of character overnight. Like any permanent structure, a character-based organization must be built brick by brick, one day at a time. However, the following three keys provide ethical business leaders with the necessary guidelines to begin.

KEY # 1 — MORAL CLARITY

First Principle: Commit to Uncompromising Ethical Standards

The first step is to recognize and believe that, although our corporate organizations operate within the capitalist model where profits are both fundamental and essential, businesses must earn those profits within the context of the "rules." In short, we must believe that robber barons, in any century, are unacceptable within the civilized business world. This deep conviction which places profits second to an "honorable name" must be consistently reflected in the words and actions of every leader within the company.

Public declaration of these beliefs, although essential, is not in itself sufficient. Corporate leaders must actively manifest character development in every aspect of their organization's functioning. This can be accomplished in two ways: 1) reward individuals who display a clear commitment to excellent character, and 2) take immediate and decisive action against those who demonstrate a lack of ethical behavior.

Corporate leaders worldwide must send a clear message

that establishes a "zero tolerance" standard for character lapses. They must also regularly communicate to all of their people that this standard is non-negotiable, profit insensitive, and most importantly—immovable and unchangeable. The message throughout the organization must be crystal clear: *Our credibility and reputation in the marketplace will depend upon excellent character and a good name; nothing less will be acceptable under any circumstances.*

Several thousand years ago, King Solomon, known for his wisdom, observed that, "A good name is more desirable than great riches; to be esteemed better than silver or gold." To translate his words into today's terms, the great riches are profits, and the silver and gold represent shareholder earnings. Nothing has changed.

Second Principle: Reconstruct from the Inside Out

New paint on the walls may temporarily change the look and smell of a room, but it does nothing to change the structure or reality. That's why our organizations do not need redecorating—they need complete corporate reconstruction. Leaders need to commit to a new blueprint, one that requires tearing out any defective structure, department, or person that contributes to the decay of ethical rationalism and replacing them with structures and people who understand inherently that no substitute will be accepted for having a "good name." Only in this manner will customers, suppliers, the investor community and the public at large once again accept and trust the word of our corporate leaders.

However, we must not only look inside our organizations during this house cleaning, but outside as well. Think about it. Why did so many corporations abandon long-standing relationships with Arthur Andersen, before its collapse, even though it would cost them more financially in the near-term to reconstruct their audit and other accounting and consulting relationships? The answer is clear. These companies realized that continued association with Andersen would tarnish their own name, even though in many cases the Andersen partners and staff that these former clients were dealing with may have been far removed from the source of the Enron/Andersen problem.

Corruption of any kind always leaves a lingering stench. Ethical corruption generates guilt by association. Just as parents commonly warn their children that others will judge them by the company they keep, business leaders must heed the same advice. One of the strongest deterrents to corporate misdeeds is isolation and the resulting economic loss. Those who associate with unethical organizations, though possibly innocent of any wrongdoings themselves, will unfortunately share in the injury of the offending party. Such is the reality of the business world.

Third Principle: Seek Wise Counsel and Be Careful Whom You Esteem

If we truly aspire to set an uncompromising moral example, then we need to also be careful whose advice we follow as well as whom we honor. For example, as the Enron/ Anderson drama continued to unfold on the main stage, a smaller, but nonetheless interesting act was being played out on a side stage of the business community. Tom Peters, a long-heralded although highly questionable business guru, was busy re-spinning a new "old story," only to withdraw it and then recast it once again. His on-again, off-again explanation as to the integrity and legitimacy of the data that formed the basis for the book *In Search of Excellence*, which he coauthored twenty years ago, is the crux of this drama.

In the December 2001 issue of *Fast Company* magazine, Peters states in an article he authored:

> Confession #3
>
> This is pretty small beer, but for what it's worth, okay, I confess: We faked the data. A lot of people suggested it at the time.... We went around to McKinsey's partners and to a bunch of other smart people who were deeply involved and seriously engaged in the world of business and asked, Who's cool? Who's doing cool work? Where is there great stuff going on? And which companies genuinely get it?
>
> Start by using common sense, by trusting your instincts, and by soliciting the views of "strange" (that is, non-conventional) people. **You can always worry about proving the facts later.**[xxxviii]
>
> *(Emphasis added)*

Then, in the February 2002 issue of the same magazine he states,

> The "fact" is, I'm well trained in math in general and in arcane statistical analysis in particular. Thus,

in, say, a DCF (discounted cash flow) project analysis, I can make most anything come out the way I want by fiddling with the discount rate or futzing with cash flow in the distant "out-years"—far beyond our knowledge. Such shenanigans are used in boardrooms every day to justify absurd mergers...

...I/we did not "fake the data" in our book. But we weren't slaves to numbers either—which was the tenor of the time.

We did use "the data"—selectively and to suit our purposes.

Analysis is mostly a prejudiced, totally subjective farce—made to look sober...[xxxix]

These statements fly in the face of every character-based organization. Of course, Peters has profited immensely over the past two decades from the book's popularity, with more than three million copies sold. If that were not enough, *BusinessWeek* quotes Peters as saying, "Get off my case, we didn't fake the data. It's called an aggressive headline."[xl]

Does such behavior demonstrate high character and exemplary leadership? Yet, despite all, many corporate leaders still flock to hear Peters and others like him. In reflection, I am reminded of something Kevin Cashman once said, "Too many people separate the act of leadership from the leader. They see leadership as something that they **do**—rather than an expression of who they **are**."

Twenty years ago we may have been "slaves to numbers" or, just maybe, twenty years ago we were far more concerned about truth and integrity. Peters' actions are a microcosm of what is wrong with corporate America. There is a loss of truthfulness. Warren Buffett, in a *New York Times* article put it succinctly, "...C.E.O.'s don't need 'independent' directors, oversight committees or auditors absolutely free of conflicts of interest. They simply need to do what is right." As Alan Greenspan forcefully declared last week, "the attitudes and actions of C.E.O's are what determine corporate conduct."[xli]

An Example of Organizational Character

Amid these discouraging reports of corporate and personal dishonor, there are organizations whose decisive commitment to act honorably makes them standard-bearers of corporate character. For instance, Mercedes Benz recently announced that it would not patent its new crash protection system for passenger cars. Why? After all, the company had spent millions of dollars in R&D to develop this breakthrough in auto safety. Because, to put it in the words of the Mercedes Benz president, "Some things are just too important not to share."

Will the company's decision cost it money? Undoubtedly, at least in the short-term, as it will suffer from lost licensing revenues from the other automakers worldwide. However, it is likely that over the long-term the value of customer goodwill generated by this decision will more than compensate for the short-term cost. Regardless, it is an example of a commitment to corporate character leading executives to do what is honorable, and in this case, helping to save many lives.

KEY # 2 — STRATEGIC CLARITY

Earlier I addressed the issue of executive leaders buying into the "lie" that high ethical standards and business are incompatible. I believe that there is a second major reason that business executives fall into ethical compromise as a result of misperceptions. In business, we tend to perceive tangible outcomes as our goal and thus focus all of our attention on achieving tangible results.

Talk with most highly motivated, competitive, success driven business leaders about the objectives they strive to achieve for their corporation and you will come up with the following list.

10 TANGIBLE outcomes

1. Profit Growth

2. Enhanced Stockholder Value

3. Business Growth

4. Increased Productivity

5. Cost Control

6. Employee Retention

7. Motivated Workforce

8. Improved Product / Service Quality

9. Cutomer Loyalty

10. Increased Market Share

When we focus all of our attention and energies on these ten tangible outcomes as the ultimate measure of our success, bending the ethical rules to gain an advantage

 **INTANGIBLE** imperatives

1. Trust

2. Personal Integrity

3. Respect

4. Dignity

5. Valuing Individuals

6. Open Communication

7. Shared Vision

8. Empowerment

9. Freedom to Contribute

10. Enhanced Self Worth

becomes a constant temptation. We need to change our primary focus away from these very tangible and desirable outcomes to ten intangible imperatives.

When we change our primary focus from achieving the tangible to accomplishing these intangible imperatives, our entire perspective changes and with it our ethical viewpoint. In so doing, we need not abandon the tangible outcomes. In fact, the opposite is true. The more we focus our time, attention and energies on the intangibles, the needs of the people around us, the better we build a solid foundation for an organization that will ultimately produce the desired tangible outcomes consistently and in abundance.

KEY # 3 — MORAL IMPERATIVE

A Commitment to Doing What is Right

Recently, President George W. Bush said, "In this era, where we expect for there to be personal responsibility in America, we expect there to be corporate responsibility as well. First, we must remember the high standards that come with high office."[xlii] Couple this with a final comment from Warren Buffett, "C.E.O.'s want to be respected and believed. They will be—and should be—only when they deserve to be."[xliii]

No external force will ever be able to compel leaders to behave in an ethical manner. The decision must be a free-will choice, rooted in moral determination. Ultimately, when it comes to developing an organization of character, what leaders say, how they act, and whom they esteem must reflect a consistent message of honor, integrity and high ethical character. The battle lines are drawn. Our free enterprise system is at stake. Will you stand? Will you fight to reclaim the ethical high ground?

I believe that corporate leaders who determine to do what is right can achieve success through significance and leave an honorable and enduring legacy.

~ JOHN DI FRANCES

POSTSCRIPT
[postscript]

A PERSONAL JOURNEY

Postscript

Postscript
A PERSONAL JOURNEY

The insights I have shared in this book are the result of thirty years of business experience, nineteen as a company owner. During this time, I have come to recognize my own strengths and weaknesses and to value the many abilities and contributions of my staff. I have also learned the benefit of good character among business associates and have personally paid the price when it is found lacking. It is my desire to pass on the truths I have learned, in many cases the hard way, to help other leaders do their jobs more effectively.

Good leaders choose to uphold high ethical standards simply because it is the right thing to do. It is important, however, to understand that there are fundamental reasons for moral behavior which supersede the mere pragmatics of what works in the marketplace. Indeed, it would be inappropriate for me to offer practical solutions, but say nothing of the foundational beliefs and experiences that have shaped my thinking. I am a Christian. I believe in the tenets set forth by the Apostles' Creed, the oldest creed in the church. It begins:

I believe in God the Father Almighty, maker of heaven and earth: And in Jesus Christ his only Son, our Lord...

Faith in God and Biblical principles have given deeper purpose to everything I do.

My greatest lessons have come from the life of Christ. Here we encounter true servant leadership quietly carried out on the dusty roads of everyday life—real people with real problems meeting Jesus and His ultimate example of "doing what's right." Here we witness the antithesis of self-aggrandizement and self-serving ambition.

I believe that corporate leaders who determine to do what is right can achieve success through significance and by doing so leave an honorable and enduring legacy. Striving for moral excellence will not ensure an easy or smooth road, but it has been my experience that God never fails to come to our aid in times of need.

We know the truth not only by the reason but also by the heart.

~ BLAISE PASCAL

ABOUT THE AUTHOR

John Di Frances' professional career spans thirty years of global corporate, nonprofit and government agency experience in senior executive and industry leadership positions.

He has been a popular speaker and authority on the subject of leadership and ethical principles since the 1980s, when he began teaching ethics courses for the Federal Government. John believes that for leadership to be effective, it must be founded on ethics and rooted in high moral principle. It is John's conviction that to establish such leadership and build an enduring positive legacy, there must be a resolute commitment to act with integrity and honor. John's new book, *Reclaiming the Ethical High Ground: Developing Organizations of Character* and his forthcoming book, *Radical Leadership*, examine the concepts of effective and ethical leadership.

Currently, John spends most of his time assisting organizations internationally through his professional speaking and executive advisory services. Addressing issues such as Leadership, Ethics, Innovation, Synergy and Negotiation, he provides organizations with a practical foundation and enables them to initiate value-driven strategies.

A 1973 Honors graduate from the University of Wisconsin, John holds a degree in Business and Economics. He has since served as a faculty member of the National Contract Management Association and has been certified as a Premier Expert by Prosavy.

John is the founder and Managing Partner of DI FRANCES & ASSOCIATES, LLC. He has also served as an outside director on corporate boards and has been retained as an expert witness in business litigations.

His career memberships have included the following:

American Bar Association
National Speakers Association
Meeting Professionals International
Turnaround Management Association
Association of Certified Fraud Examiners
National Contract Management Association
American Defense Preparedness Association
Wisconsin Professional Speakers Association
National Defense Industrial Association
Association of the United States Army
United States Naval Institute

John and his wife, Sally, live at their home, Blackberry Hill, in Genesee, Wisconsin, just outside the Milwaukee metro area. They are the parents of five, four daughters and a son.

DI FRANCES & ASSOCIATES, LLC

John Di Frances is founder and Managing Partner of DI FRANCES & ASSOCIATES, LLC, a firm assisting organizations internationally through executive advisory services. John is also a professional speaker. The firm specializes in aiding corporate, government, non-profit and educational/religious organizations in developing value-driven strategies for more effective leadership and operations.

DI FRANCES & ASSOCIATES, LLC has worked with international organizations since 1983, ranging from aerospace and defense to pharmaceutical; "black" (secret) weapons programs and high technology to consumer products; engineering and construction to computers, software and systems as well as religious and philanthropic foundations.

Clients have included the U.S. Government, major U.S. corporations such as United Defense, Merck/Medco Pharmaceutical, and United Technologies Corporation as well as numerous offshore corporations, trusts and foundations in Europe and Asia.

In addition, DI FRANCES & ASSOCIATES, LLC's web site offers a variety of helpful resources, including a complimentary electronic newsletter, free access to John Di Frances' article archive, books and learning/training materials.

For information about these resources, or to learn more about DI FRANCES & ASSOCIATES, LLC, please visit:

http://www.difrances.com

Or contact the firm directly at:

208 East Oak Crest Drive, Suite 200,
Wales, WI 53183-9700 U.S.A.

Phone: 262.968.9850 Fax: 262.968.9854
Email: info@difrances.com

END NOTES

[i]President George W. Bush, speech to Wall Street, 9 July 2002.

[ii]"Paul Volcker on the Crises of Faith," NEWSMAKER Q&A, *BusinessWeek* [online], 14 June 2002.

[iii]"Reforming Corporate America." *Newsweek*, MSNBC, 20 June 2002.

[iv]David Leonhardt, "The Imperial Chief Is Suddenly in the Cross Hairs," *The New York Times*, 24 June 2002.

[v]"If Only CEO Meant Chief Ethical Officer," *BusinessWeek* [online], 13 June 2002.

[vi]National Press Club luncheon, 5 June 2002.

[vii]David Leonhardt, "The Imperial Chief Is Suddenly in the Cross Hairs."

[viii]"Treasury Secretary Condemns Corporate Scandals," *Bloomburg News*, 23 June 2002.

[ix]David Leonhardt, "The Imperial Chief Is Suddenly in the Cross Hairs."

[x]James C. Young, *Harvey S. Firestone 1868-1938* (Chicago: The Lakeside Press, R.R. Donnelley & Sons Company, 1938).

[xi]Lawrence W. Reed, *A Lesson from the Past – The Silver Panic of 1893* (New York: The Foundation for Economic Education, Inc., Irving-on-Hudson).

[xii]President Grover Cleveland, speech to a Special Session of the Congress in response to the Silver Panic, 8 August 1893.

[xiii]Ken Brown and Ianthe Jeanne Dugan, *The Wall Street Journal*, 7 June 2002.

[xiv]"Paul Volcker on the Crises of Faith."

[xiv]"Merrill Lynch to Pay Big Fine, Increase Oversight of Analysts," *The Wall Street Journal*, 22 May 2002.

[xvi]President George W. Bush, speech to Wall Street.

[xvii]"Reforming Corporate America," *Newsweek*, MSNBC, 20 June 2002.

[xviii]"Reforming Corporate America," *Newsweek*, MSNBC.

[xix]Leslie Wayne, "Corporate Integrity Talk is Heard in Street and Suite," *The New York Times*, 10 July 2002.

[xx]President George W. Bush, speech to Wall Street.

[xxi]Securities and Exchange Commission news release , 14 June 2000.

[xxii]David Leonhardt, "The Imperial Chief Is Suddenly in the Cross Hairs."

[xxiii]Ken Brown and Ianthe Jeanne Dugan, *The Wall Street Journal*, 7 June 2002.

[xxiv]Berkshire Hathaway web site, (www.berkshirehathaway.com), 2002.

[xxv]FedEx web site, (www.fedex.com), 2002.

[xxvi]Chemistry information courtesy of 3M Corporate Media Relations

[xxvii]Courtesy of Midwest Express Airlines

[xxviii]Wendy's International web site, (www.wendys.com), 2002.

[xxix]Dave Thomas, *Well Done! The Common Guy's Guide to Everyday Success* (Grand Rapids: Zondervan Publishing House, 1994).

[xxx]ServiceMaster web site, (www.servicemaster.com), 2002.

[xxxi]Excerpted from John Di Frances' forthcoming book, *Radical Leadership*, Reliance Books

In recording the true story of Major General John Buford's activities on the days of June 30th through July 1st, 1863, I have relied upon numerous resources, most notably, *The American Heritage Picture History of the Civil War*, Editor in Charge Richard M. Ketchum with Narrative by Bruce Catton, American Heritage Publishing Company, Inc., *Battles and Leaders of the Civil War – The Tide Shifts*, Volume III, Edited by Robert Underwood Johnson and Clarence Clough Buel, Castle, *Generals In Blue – Lives of the Union Commanders*, Ezra J. Warner, Louisiana State University Press, *Gettysburg: The Final Fury with Maps and Illustrations*, Bruce Catton, Doubleday & Company, Inc., *The Killer Angels*, Michael Shaara, David McKay Company, Inc., *Witness To Gettysburg*, Richard Wheeler, Harper & Row Publishers.

[xxxii]James C. Young, *Harvey S. Firestone 1868-1938*.

[xxxiii]"Where Can execs Learn Ethics? News Analysis," *BusinessWeek* [online], 13 June 2002.

[xxxiv]General Charles Krulak, Commandant, United States Marine Corps, speech at the annual Joint Services Conference on Ethics (JSCOPE), 27 January 2000.

[xxxv]President George W. Bush, speech to Wall Street, 9 July 2002.

[xxxvi]David Leonhardt, "The Imperial Chief Is Suddenly in the Cross Hairs."

[xxxvii]Joann s. Lublin and Carol Hymowitz, "Fearing Scandals, Executives Spurn CEO Job Offers," *The Wall Street Journal*, 27 June 2002.

[xxxviii]Tom Peters, "Tom Peter's True Confessions," *Fast Company*, December 2001.

[xxxix]Tom Peters, "Tom Peter's True Confessions," *Fast Company*, February 2002.

[xl]"We faked the data? Tom Peters Explains," *BusinessWeek*, 3 December, 2001.

[xli]Warren E. Buffett, "Who Really Cooks the Books?" *The New York Times*, 24 July, 2002.

[xlii]Howard Fineman, "The Politics of Greed," *Newsweek*, MSNBC, 1 July, 2002.

[xliii]Warren E. Buffett, "Who Really Cooks the Books?" *The New York Times*, 24 July 2002.

INDEX

D

E

READER RESPONSE FORM

If you have enjoyed reading *Reclaiming the Ethical High Ground: Developing Organizations of Character* we would like to hear from you. Please photocopy this page and fax it back to us. We would like to assist you in any manner that we can.

Contact Information:

Comments:

Requests:

☐   Please send additional information on DI FRANCES & ASSOCIATES, LLC's services.

Fax back to 262.968.9854